POM

BASKETMAKING

A Supreme Art

For The Weaver

by Elsie Allen

Edited by Vinson Brown

Naturegraph Publishers, Inc., Happy Camp, California 96039

DEDICATION

To my Mother, and to all other weavers

of Pomo baskets, past, present, and in the

future.

Books for a better world

1988 Edition.

Paper Edition: ISBN 0-87961-016-6;   Cloth Edition: ISBN 0-87961-017-4

THE OLD TEACHER AND THE YOUNG LEARNER

Mrs. Annie Burke, mother of Mrs. Elsie Allen, showing a young Pomo Indian relative how to work on a lattice weave, number 4 twine basket. Photo taken in Hopland, California, about 1935. Unfortunately, the young learners are few and far between today, as the young Indian girls grow up in the white man's culture and use easy-to-get manufactured items. We hope that soon more people will come to know the deep and rich satisfaction that comes from learning and perfecting this ancient and extremely beautiful art of the Pomo people.

PREFACE

The Pomo Indians had a unique feeling in the old days for the earth and its life that we need to understand. Understanding will help us appreciate the beauty and goodness of this land we live in and fill us with the desire to help preserve that beauty from its destruction.

Take a Pomo Basketweaver, for example. She worked constantly with sky and earth and living plants and with great patience and devotion to create something of superlative beauty, a tribute to the harmony of man with the universe. She watched the sky and also felt the sky, its changing moods and its signs of what was coming, so that she knew by the literal feel of the air, something reaching into her inner being, that now was a good time to make a trip to the eastern mountains to collect the reddish bark of the Redbud Tree, a bark that could be made into strips and used to weave beautiful red designs onto the sides of baskets.

Another day would come, probably in late February, when she felt the warmth of an early spring rising as an ethereal flavor out of the warm earth and the smell of young green growing things, and these signs would tell her that the sedge roots in the marshy and low spots near rivers or other large streams were growing now with wild abandon beneath the soil. Now they could be dug up from that soil to be made into basket coils; to weave around willow withes found at an earlier date.

In digging for those roots, or touching the willow twigs and the Redbud bark, her fingertips told her many stories out of the womb and the matrix of Mother Earth. They told her when the sandy loam in which the sedge roots grow was getting thicker and more easily dug, thus providing growing room for the very longest roots, ones especially prized by basketweavers. Bark touch—smooth or rough—told her when to strip the bark. Wood strength and give, in willow branchlets, told her when the willow was just right to be cut and formed into a basket's skeleton.

When all the days and months of creating a basket went past—the warm days of digging, the soft touch of the earth, the good feel of the root strips, the watching of them drying in the sun, the exact splitting of the sedge roots to make the final basket weave, the wetting of just the right amount to make them resilient when weaving, the weave itself rising into beauty under her fingers, the final touch of bright bird feathers, woodpecker and duck, bluebird and oriole—she felt a music of harmony with all living things and with the Spirit that is quite unique.

—Vinson Brown

TABLE OF CONTENTS AND ILLUSTRATIONS

(2) Elsie Allen and Finished Baby Basket
Photo by Robert Cooper

I

THE LIFE OF ELSIE ALLEN, POMO BASKETWEAVER

Elsie Allen is well known today for her basketweaving art. This art was handed down to her by her mother and her mother's mother before her from a long line of Pomo Indian basket weavers who lived on this good earth of Sonoma, Mendocino and Lake Counties in California for thousands of years. Her ancestors knew every hill and canyon, every river and spring. They felt akin to every tree, shrub and flower, animal, bird and insect. Even the rocks were part of their heritage. Elsie's story tells us about some of this heritage in this last 70 odd years.

I was born near Santa Rosa on September 22, 1899, at a time which was very bad for my people. During the previous one hundred years the white people had come by wagon trains—in groups from the south and the north, bringing disease, war and destruction to our way of life until we had become a few little bands of people huddled here and there in what had once been our country, fighting to stay alive by working for the ranchers usually at sheepshearing or wood chopping and in the hopfields.

My parents were George and Annie Comanche, and I was baptised Elsie Comanche at the just being built Catholic Church in Santa Rosa.

But I have no proof of my birth, as it was recorded only in the Catholic Church and this was lost. We were all nominal Catholics, but seldom saw a priest as we lived too far away from where there was a church. Some old religious beliefs of the Pomo people we carried into the new religion of the Catholic Church, and one of these was fasting. We fasted for many things, for example we would fast before starting work on a basket such as a red feather or woodpecker feather basket and would work at it as long as possible and then when we were too hungry we would eat but no longer work on the basket. The fasting was for purification so as to receive help from the Great Spirit in whatever we did.

I lived with my grandmother in my very early years. This was in the Cloverdale area. Cloverdale of course at that time was a small village with one main store that served the nearby ranches. We lived a rather isolated existence and since I had no toys or playmates, rocks and leaves served well to build houses and to make doll people. Wormwood was a favorite for doll people, the tips being good to bend over for hair. It was fun to climb Madrone trees for leaves that the leaf miners were busy designing. It was fun also walking through the water of a swift stream hunting cattail-like grass. The muddy roots were cleaned off and it became hair for other doll people. Elderberry bushes, willows and other trees were named as persons and given a personality in my imagination. Othertimes I would run through the animal trails in the Chamise brush with my mother's fox terrier. We would run and run for simply hours. Before we would start running the dog would jump around and run ahead of me and turn around as if to say "Come on, Hurry up!" Sometimes I would run a different way and when the dog missed me he would come back and look for me. He was as happy as I to have a playmate and was a favorite pet along with a kitty I treasured. These playtimes gave me an appreciation of nature, but of course all this isolation made me overly shy even among children of my own age.

We suffered much from the diseases of the white people in those early days. I was very sick with the measles when I was five years of age. Since no white doctors were available, we used many healing herbs. I remember when sick at this time having nightmares of giant roosters walking about me and crowing at me so that I was very frightened. When I was about six my grandfather, an Indian singing doctor, told my

parents that he could protect me from most diseases by a special
ceremony. He built a very hot fire and threw a live turtle into it which
was killed instantly by the heat. It was then pulled out by some long
stick tongs, and I was given its hot blood to drink. I kept choking on
it, but finally got the stuff down. It is possible this may have saved me
from tuberculosis later, as when I was at the Indian school in Covelo at
the age of eleven, and was very sad and lonely an older Indian girl
who had tuberculosis befriended me. She gradually got so sick she had
to stay in bed and I was given the job of taking her food to her. She
ate so lightly that much of it was left. As I was near to starving in those
days because of being too shy to grab for food in a hurry on the table
as the other children did, I was helped greatly by being able to eat all
that left-over food of the sick girl. But I never caught TB because of
this, even though I used the same spoon! This food probably kept me
strong and prevented me from getting sick in other ways.

My father died when I was about eight and my mother soon after
that married Mr. Richard Burke, who was half-Pomo and half-English.
He took us north to live near Hopland and he was a very kind step-father
to me. There we lived with my great uncle and grandmother and great-
grandmother on a ranch, in a small 3-room house. My great uncle worked on a ranch near Cloverdale. In the summer we moved down by the
river and built a kind of hut like our people had in the old days, a house
made of leaves put over willow frames. We cut the willows down and
wove them over posts, then covered this with leaves. The roof of our
house was made from willow branches set across the roof top and smaller
willow twigs were woven in and out to form a solid roof to keep the
hot sun out. We had two different rooms for bedrooms, and in one my
grandmother built me a bed that was high off the ground on cross-
pieces of willow resting on four large stakes put into the ground. She
made a mattress out of corn husks and fine straw put into a bed tick,
and placed it on top of my bed. It was so high that I had to climb up
on a box to get into it. This was to keep it out of reach of snakes.

My great uncle worked in the vineyards and also helped with the
cows and horses and the haying. There were no hops in Cloverdale at
that time. He used to help also with the milking. Down near the Asti
winery they had a summer resort where my grandmother worked by

helping with the washing. My mother used to hide me or make me hide whenever the white people came because we had heard of Indian children who had been kidnapped. We usually hid in the bushes. My great-grandmother said that when she was young a number of Indian children were brought down from the north by whites, riding on mules. Her aunt fed about seven or eight of these small children who were being carried south and then to be sold to ranchers. They were so starved they swallowed their food whole. My people wept when these children were taken away for they feared they would be treated badly.

We continued to live in a wood house during the cold months, but went down to the river to live in a willow and brush house during the summer. We bought flour and sugar and other items from the store and used a wood stove to cook upon which I preferred to the old ways of my grandmother who cooked by an open fire such foods as ground acorns, pinole (a ground up wheat), deer meat and fish, and other gathered foods. We also fished and hunted for game and gathered acorns from the oaks nearby in the fall, and then ground and leached the acorns to make into acorn mush. Today I like acorn mush so much that I gather the acorns by the sackful every fall.

I had received no education up until I was eleven and it was in that year that I was taken away from my family and sent to Covelo in northeastern Mendocino County, where there was an Indian Reservation with an Indian school. A government agent came to see us and talked my mother into letting me go to that place, which was about 80 miles away from where we lived. In those days there were no highways or buses and I had to travel through the wilderness of pines and firs most of the way. Six other Indian children from the Hopland-Ukiah area travelled with me. First I went on a wagon to Ukiah and then we were all put on a flat-bed railroad car of the Northwestern Pacific Railroad and carried by the train to wooded Sherwood Valley where we changed to a stagecoach that carried us north to Laytonville, where we stayed overnight. The next day a gravel wagon picked us up to take us to Covelo. I remember being frightened by the big river, the Eel, and of the giant trees we rode under, which I thought at any minute would fall down on me. I was very tempted to jump out of the wagon and run away.

At the Covelo Indian school they placed me in a dormitory with other Indian girls. At that time I could not yet speak English, and soon

found myself unable to follow simple dressing and eating chores of the
daily existence because we children were not supposed to speak Indian,
a rule of most government Indian schools at that time. I had learned
the middle Pomo dialect to proficiency. At first there was only one
girl there I really knew and she was put in a different age group so I did
not see her very often. They tried to keep me busy by giving me cards
that had holes in them through which I was supposed to twist some
yarn. It seemed so useless. Worst of all this dormitory was burned
down one night, the fire believed to have been started by some older
girls who hated the school, and I lost nearly all my clothes that my
mother had so carefully packed and sent with me.

We had to move to a boy's dormitory and there I was forced to
wear boy's clothes. We were given various duties to do, but it was hard
for me to understand and sometimes I was punished when I did them
wrong because of lack of understanding of the language. Finally I was
given one dress, but I could not read the label on it and it looked so
much like other dresses that when I picked out what I thought was my
dress and put it on another girl would often come up very mad and take
it away from me. In time I learned to wait until every girl had taken her
dress and then figure out mine was the last one there and take it. We
usually did our work in the morning, then cleaned up at noon and put
on our school clothes to go to classes where I seemed to learn nothing
at all. My stay at Covelo was not very fruitful because of this language
barrier, and I often cried at night with homesickness.

It was so good to get home after that useless school that I follow-
ed my mother around wherever she went for days just to feel near to
her. When I was thirteen the government opened a school for Indian
children on the Rancheria where I lived near Hopland. A teacher came
there daily and fortunately she was kind and patient about the language
problem so I finally began to learn how to read, write and talk English.
I went to school there about three years.

Around this time the Sisters of Saint Dominick came to the reservation to teach the Catholic Faith. Their dark clothes and white faces
frightened me at first, but gradually I got used to them, and even began
to think maybe I should become a nun, but my mother strongly ob-
jected. This did make me feel that when I had children I would not
prevent them from doing what they wanted to do.

I started working in the hopfields when I was ten years old and during my teens to help add to our family income. This was very hot work during the summer and eventually I decided I wanted to learn something better. So at eighteen I visited one of the Catholic priests in Ukiah, whom we liked, and asked him about different kinds of jobs. He took me to San Francisco to visit the St. Joseph's Hospital, which I liked very much and would have liked to work there. But instead he took me to two elderly ladies who needed help. I started my first job at about $35.00 a month with room and board. I was never allowed out on the street alone so that after three months I began to feel like I was a prisoner in confinement and told them I wanted to quit. Angrily they packed my suitcase, flung open the front door, and told me to go.

Out in the street in San Francisco at eighteen years of age, I really felt lost at first, but soon found a streetcar heading for the Ferry Building and started traveling. From there a very helpful policeman directed me to the Saint Joseph's Hospital. Since it was the last year of the First World War, 1918, and there was a shortage of help, the hospital officials gladly offered me a job. I worked there happily for six months and was given the additional job of taking other employees to St. Boniface Church on Sunday morning and to Golden Gate Park for an outing in the afternoon to hear the band concerts at the park. My employers thought I knew my way about the city, but actually I got along fine by asking questions of conductors and policemen I met.

But just as I was getting to do my work well in the hospital pantry with chances for advancement I came down with the prevailing flu, and had to be sent home. At home I might have starved because my stomach would not hold down any regular food, but I was saved by my mother cooking me lots of acorn mush, which was so bland that it stayed down and nourished me back to health.

On May 1, 1919 I married my present husband, Arthur Allen, a northern Pomo, in a ceremony at Saint Mary's Catholic Church in Ukiah. After the Christian ceremony, he and his family came to my mother's place near Hopland for a traditional style Indian wedding. Blankets, hankerchiefs and similar gifts were given to my mother and step-father, while my family gave his family baskets full of Indian clam-shell money, ground down and pierced so the individual shells could be hung on strings like necklaces.

Our first child was Genevieve, who was born on July 31, 1920, the year we moved to the Pinoleville Indian Rancheria near a ranch on which Arthur worked. Leonard, the second baby, was born on March 10, 1922, while the third, Dorothy, was born on December 15, 1924, in Hopland. These three were all born only with the help of a midwife. My last baby was George, born on February 28, 1928.

In the time when our children were young we were so sure that only English would be of use to them in later life that most of the time we talked only English in front of them so that was the only language they learned. Now we are not so sure and are beginning to feel it is sad they did not learn their own native tongue. In 1932 we voted on the reservation to have our children go to school with the whites and this was probably good in getting them to know about the other race first hand, an experience we had not had as children.

During the years up to the age of 62, I worked at many jobs, including various harvestings of crops, and finally in a laundry after my children had grown up. But somewhere within me was the urge to come back to basketmaking. My mother and my grandmother worked at basketweaving when I was a child. When I was older I gathered sedge roots, willows, bulrushes and redbud at the same places she did such as Dry Creek Road, Mill Creek Road and in Guerneville where the Hacienda Resort is today and with the help of my mother and grandmother we cured the material and made it into baskets. However my grandmother died in 1924, so not only did I lose her help, but most of her examples of baskets as well as it was customary for an Indian woman to have all her baskets and reeds buried with her.

In the first few years of my married life, I attempted basketweaving. I made a basket of about eight or nine inches and that was buried with my grandmother. My next one-stick coiled basket was buried with my great uncle. A third basket was passed all around to relatives when someone died and finally somehow came back to us and was buried with my brother-in-law. I didn't have a good feeling about making baskets after that. Mother told me that she did not want this to happen with her as she wanted me to have her baskets to help me when I started up basketweaving again. So I promised her I would do this. Mother showed baskets for seven years. She showed baskets at the Boonville Fair, and around. She liked people and noticed how people liked the basket displays. She wanted me to travel and meet people through the baskets and not destroy her baskets and have nothing left for me and others in the future. Mother died in 1962, and I have tried to keep my promise.

Unfortunately some of my Pomo people were not pleased with me for doing this and even some of my own family came to me and told me I should stop doing it. They felt these old ways should die and we should forget the past heritage. Perhaps they thought the people would laugh at us for taking up things our ancestors once did, and some were afraid if other people learned to make baskets like the Pomo they would sell them and get rich from our art. Even one white gentleman came and told me I should not do it because it would destroy a lot of plants. He did not understand what I knew very well that the cutting out of roots and trimming of shrubs actually helped spread the growth and there was no danger as long as the digging and cutting was not overdone at any one place.

Also I felt very strongly that my people who opposed my basketmaking were wrong and were letting fears overcome their better sense, as how could we ever bring back an understanding of our own background and the beautiful things our old people did if we did not revive some of these arts. I am hoping that more and more of my people are now beginning to understand that this is really true. I was helped in my determination to be a basket weaver and have pride in my work and in my people by an experience that happened to me when I was fifty. My daughter visited me and invited me to go with her to a Chinese restaurant where I expected to see none but Chinese eating. I was amazed to see other races eating there and saw also how proud the Chinese were of their heritage. Since I felt that the Pomos were one of the greatest basket weavers in the world I resolved in my heart that this wonderful art should not be lost and that I would learn it well and teach others.

When I was 62 years of age I finally found the time I was seeking to start my basketweaving again. I went out and dug the roots and gathered the willows and hunted around for the beautiful twigs of redbud myself. I have been able to create many fine baskets from those as small as a dime up to large storage baskets and including some of the famous feather baskets that made the Pomos renowned. There is a rich and beautiful feeling to have these useful and lovely baskets grow into being under the work of your own hands and the designs that grow with them. From 1969 to August 1971 I finished 54 baskets.

In the last four years I have taught the art of basketweaving at Mendocino Art Center in Mendocino City. Several weekends in the spring are set aside to teach the students how to gather material and later on they are shown how to cure and finally weave the baskets. I would have from eight to sixteen students. I didn't attract many Indian girls as they did not like to dig in the mud. I am happy to teach all and would be especially happy if some local Indian girls would become interested in learning this art.

Basketweaving needs dedication and interest and increasing skill and knowledge; it needs feeling and love and honor for the great weavers of the past who showed us the way. If you can rouse in yourself this interest, feeling and dedication, you also can create matchless beauty and help me renew something that should never be lost.

The photograph below shows a typical streamside woodland of the California Coast Range. Here is where California Indians found most of their materials for making baskets. Willow, cottonwood and alder are generally the trees found closest to the water. The fast-growing willows furnish a plentiful and continuous supply of willow withes for the basket frameworks. Not all streamsides, however, have the proper conditions for growing bulrushes and sedges, whose roots are abundantly used in Pomo basketry. It is necessary to find places along streams where the current is not too swift so that enough sandy soil has been allowed to accumulate in low areas near the river's edge or streamside for these plants to grow. Such places should be marked on a map whenever found so that you can come back to them to gather the sedge and bulrush roots at intervals of about three years. This pruning of the sedge roots in the ground every three years is actually good for the plants, preventing the roots from growing so thick they overuse the nutrients in the soil and preventing the roots from growing into tangled masses that are so hard on basketweaving diggers!

See illustrations on page 21 of the four kinds of plants used in basketweaving.

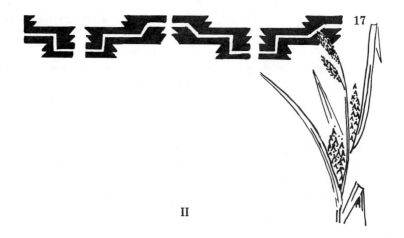

II

GATHERING MATERIALS FOR USE IN POMO BASKETWEAVING

This can be either an adventure and lots of fun, or drudgery and hard work, depending on how you look at it. In the old days, the time of going out to gather basket materials was undertaken by Pomo Indian women and girls with much the same happiness and anticipation as going on a picnic. Usually they chose nice, sunny days so that the trips down along the creeks and rivers looking for sedge roots, willow withes and bulrushes, or up into the eastern hills to find redbud twigs, were times of adventure, much laughter, and bantering, as well as hard work when the right materials were found. The work, however, which involved the handling and cutting of plant materials and the digging for roots in the warm earth in springtime, gave a feeling of being a part of the beautiful natural world. It was healthful and invigorating, a good muscle- and nerve-building tonic, while the warm, delightful hours passed till the time came to pause and have a good belly-filling picnic lunch of acorn meal mush, roots, tubers, and maybe a cooked rabbit or rat. And all about, the birds were singing and many interesting animals or insects could be watched—especially by the children, who helped their mothers only until they got tired.

WILLOWS

These vary in color from gray to white. White withes, or twigs, are picked and cut in short or long lengths for use in different size baskets. They are gathered usually in the spring when the leaves first appear, or in the fall. Long straight twigs not more than one-half inch thick are best.

Preparation of each twig for use in basketry is the hardest part. They are whittled when fresh or dry to the size needed for a basket, taking days or a week to clean, strip, whittle, sort into sizes, and then dry them for two or three hot days in the sun. A pocket knife or sharp kitchen knife is used to strip the willows of bark and then scrape them to an even size or thickness for each length of willow. This must be done, for in their natural state they are thick at one end and thin at the other. Some basket-makers use a broken piece of glass or a fine sandpaper to give a smooth finish to each length. When each willow is the correct even thickness, groups are tied in bundles according to thickness and length, and then hung out to dry. After drying, they are stored in a dry place to be used in basketmaking one year later.

An awl is used to separate the spaces between each coiled root (of the sedge and the willows) when working on the basket, making it easier to put your root through the basket. A useful awl with a sharp steel point can be obtained at a hardware store. In the old days, the Indians

 used a bone awl, which was shaped to a fine point and polished slick as glass for separating basket weaves. The handle was often made to fit in the palm of the hand, making it easier to hold. Today these old-time awls are scarce among the Indian tribes, as only a few older women have kept up their basketweaving.

ROOTS

White sedge roots or bulrush roots are dug from the sandy soil by a creek, marsh or river, generally in early spring. A three-pronged curved fork was used in the old days, and a similar steel fork for digging can be used today, or even a trowel. Your hands and fingernails also help a lot in separating a long root from the soil. Be very careful not to break the roots any more than can be prevented, because the longer a root is, the easier it is to use in basketmaking. One advantage of going back every second year—or at least every third year—to a good root-digging place is that you keep the roots from getting over abundant and tangled and thus hard to dig. When the roots are tangled—as they are in most long-untouched places—they are very hard to untangle, especially as you must try to keep them long, not allowing them to break into short pieces. When you run into roots of other plants, you should take them out so the sedge roots can grow without competition, much as you weed a garden. When there are many mixed roots, the Indian women must labor for hours to get out the long good roots. Possibly this is why Indian men seldom took part in such root digging! However, as certain root areas or gardens are cultivated regularly every two or three years, the roots become longer and longer and easier to get out. Permission may be needed to dig roots in some areas, but you can assure the landowner that you are actually improving his land by doing the digging, as the sedge roots grow back quickly after being taken out—as long as you leave some in the ground—and they are of great help in holding the soil along creeks and rivers.

The sedge roots are hard to find now in quantity or of good quality because they have been disturbed by too many roads and buildings, but man needs to learn that the sedge root is a vital part of the harmony of nature and preserving of the soil. It is especially useful in preventing creek banks from washing away, and can be encouraged to grow by all property owners. Digging of the roots, when correctly done and leaving behind about half of those found, actually strengthens the growth and soil-holding properties of the roots.

White sedge roots have an outer bark. A split is started with a sharp knife along the center of each root and the entire length of the root carefully and evenly divided into two equal halves. The outer bark is then peeled off and the cleaned roots are coiled for drying, which takes about six months. When one is ready to weave a basket, she soaks a few roots in water for half an hour, then scrapes them clean and very smooth with a knife, leaving the center side flat and the outer side round. (The flat side will lie against the willow, and the round side is the outer part that shows in the basketwork.) The old-timers prepare their roots by holding one end of a root between their teeth with the other end in their left hand. Then they hold, in their right hand, a short piece of root doubled around the main root, and move this short piece back and forth against the tightly held main root until all excess matter falls loose from it. This process is done beautifully by the old Indians who have the nack, but a knife can be used with equal success.

Be sure, however, that before all this finishing and cleaning work is done, the roots are coiled and dried properly. This very important process will take from six months to a year, depending upon the climate. Hang the roots in a dry place and watch carefully to see that they stay dry.

Black root is the dyed bulrush root. It is stronger than the sedge root and is brownish in color. It cannot be used in place of white sedge root as the main weave of the basket, but it is excellent to use in designs, along with the reddish redbud twigs which make the reddish designs.

The bulrush can be dyed when it is fresh or later when dried. It takes three to six months to obtain the true black color by soaking these roots—how long depends on the weather. When the weather is hot, it takes about three months. The dye that is put on these roots does not fade and is a very dark color, from which the rush root, as used in the basket, gets its name of "black root."

The black dye is made by soaking black walnuts, rusty metal and ashes in water. The brown stems of the bulrush are soaked in this mixture until the dye is fixed. After the dye is made, the roots of the bulrush are soaked in a large five-gallon tin half full of the walnuts, metal and ashes, and into which rainwater is poured to the brim. It may be necessary to let the dye grow in strength for some months before putting the bulrush roots into it to be dyed.

Redbud twigs are gathered in the winter around the last of October. They are used to make a red design on the baskets. These have to be quite thin twigs to be approximate in size to the sedge roots used for the bulk of the basket. They are cut, split and dried as with the sedge roots, and then each twig must be scraped down with a knife to thin it out to be equal in thickness throughout the length. It is then hung up to dry in the hot sun and stored in groups of similar size, like the sedge roots.

Redbud is a small tree of the inner coast ranges, which are drier than those near the sea, and where this plant is a part of the chaparral, or California brush forests. Be careful not to hurt the trees from which you cut small branches, making the cuts clean and taking only a small or very moderate number of branches.

Baskets using these materials do not need polish or wax when finished, but they are left in a natural state, and without any painting.

(NOTE: People who have land where sedge roots grow can allow basket-weavers to gather roots, provided that they don't leave any litter and that they leave about half the roots to reproduce. Please let local Indians or the publishers know if you have land that might be used for root gathering.)

COMMON PLANTS USED IN POMO BASKETRY

WILLOW

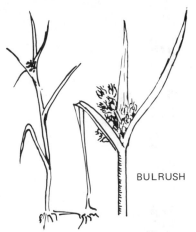

BULRUSH

The willow (*Salix* species) is found growing along stream banks. Those with white or greyish bark are best for basketry. The twigs should be cut off in early spring or in late fall.

The Bulrush (*Scirpus pacificus*) is common in many damp localities. especially in marshes or near streams. The brown root, used in basketry, is a horizontal rhizome that extends a long way near the underground surface. It grows from 3 to 9 feet tall.

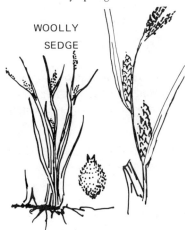

WOOLLY
SEDGE

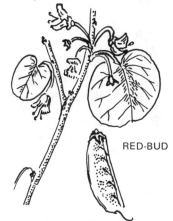

RED-BUD

Most sedge grasses have roots usable for basketweaving. The one shown is the Woolly Sedge (*Carex lanuginosa*). They are found in damp sandy soil near streams and marshes. Sedge grasses can be identified by their triangular-shaped stems, and they grow to about 2-3½ feet tall.

The California Redbud (*Cercis occidentalis*) is a large shrub or small tree 8-15 feet high that grows in the dry inner Coast Range or on the foothills of the Sierras. Its reddish-colored twigs are best gathered for baskets in the fall.

III

POMO INDIAN BASKET DESIGNS

Early Pomo Indians always had basket designs in black and white, except when they used redbud twigs. The Pomos didn't use human figures in designs, as this was taboo to them. Many old Indian designs show a spiral line of white between black pigments. Today these old designs are frequently used, but some weavers make new designs. Usually the design done in black was begun on the seventh round of a coiled basket, sometimes sooner or sometimes later, depending on the size of the basket.

Spanish beads (called Indian beads by Americans) are used in some baskets. Each bead is strung through the sedge root individually with every stitch and is worked in different colors to create designs.

A number of pictures of baskets are shown in this book to illustrate various designs and types. The descriptions of the baskets shown are given under each picture. You may wish to study these pictures carefully to get ideas of design and type of baskets you might like to make. Remember, however, you can use your imagination to make and design baskets that are uniquely your own. (Note: it is taboo or forbidden for a Pomo to copy a Medicine Woman's designs in making a basket.)

(4) In the picture above, Mrs. Elsie Allen holds two medium-sized coiled baskets in her hands. The largest of the two is a one-stick coiled basket with arrowhead design, while the smaller is a three-stick coiled basket of ant trail design. To the right of Mrs. Allen is a large one-stick twine basket used as a burden basket in the old days by the men for carrying heavy burdens. On her left is a winnowing or fanning twine basket. This was used by the women to winnow out edible seeds from wild plants, particularly grasses. The photograph was taken by Brooks Otis.

(5) The picture above shows a small winnowing basket being used to hold live caterpillars, which were cooked and eaten by the Pomo in ancient times. Photo reproduced by permission of the Lowie Museum of Anthropology, Berkeley, California.

(6) (Below) Type of Feather Basket.

(7) The above picture is of Mrs. Annie Burke, Elsie's mother, holding a lattice weave twine basket of storage type. Notice the way the willow has been made into a strong rim around the top of this large basket. Such a basket might be used to store acorns in the old days.

(8) The basket shown below is the largest I've seen, appearing to be about four feet high. It was made at Ukiah by Nellie Burke in 1898. It is a number 3 type twined basket, probably used for storage. Larger baskets are difficult to make, and therefore are more valuable. It takes two to three months of steady work, day after day, to make a basket about five inches wide and three inches deep, with the diameter at the top of about four inches, which explains to some extent the great value of these baskets.

IV

HOW TO MAKE COILED BASKETS

Coiled baskets are probably the most recent kind developed by the Pomo, and also the most sophisticated. It is the three-stick (or willow) coil basket that can be made so tightly that it can hold water better than any other basket. This is also the kind of basket type that is used for the world famous Pomo Feather Baskets (see pages 24, 34, 35, and 38).

The Single Stick Coil Basket

This is also called the one-stick basket and is made by the following steps, first illustrated with drawings and then with photographs.

(a) Four sedge roots (each actually a sedge root half, made when a single root was split down the middle) are tied together in a knot as shown above to start a basket.

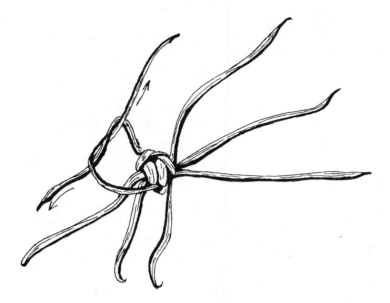

(b) In the second step two of the roots are tied again as shown above to increase the size of the knot. (You may notice that each root has its end sharpened to a point by a knife so it can slip easily into the holes between roots or willows.)

(c) Below the knot of sedge roots is thickened by continuing this tying of each set of two roots in turn.

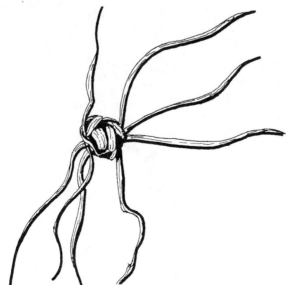

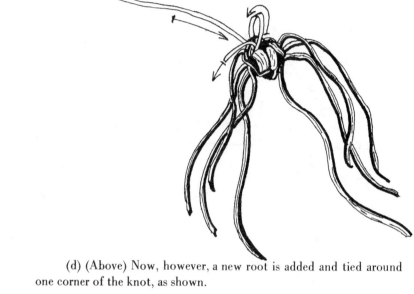

(d) (Above) Now, however, a new root is added and tied around one corner of the knot, as shown.

(e) (Below) This starts a curving section of wrapped-around knots, making the beginning of a circular coil.

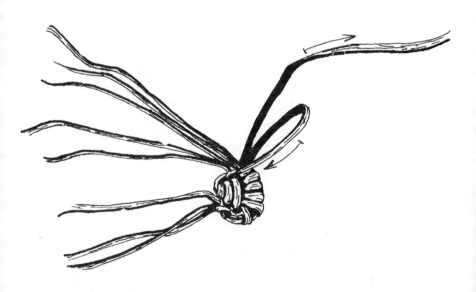

(f) When little more than a circle is completed with this coil, a willow stem is spliced into the end of the coil by driving its point in to match the point of the last-used sedge root so the two can be wrapped together. Care must be taken to make each wrapping tight. An awl is used to punch holes for the root point to enter, as it is now coiled around the single willow, attaching it to the outer coil of roots (see photograph number 24 for how an awl is used).

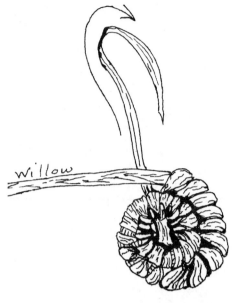

(g) Shown here is the continuation of the beginning of a one-willow coiled basket, with it coiling around the center and being woven to the previous coil very tightly. This coiling is continued on a flat plain until the bottom of the basket is formed. Then the coils are gradually tightened, drawing up the sides of the basket until it reaches the top. The top can either be straight up or incurved, depending on the intended use of the basket.

To end the final coil and make a smooth flat top, trim down the end of the last willow in the coil to a sharp point and wrap tightly with roots until snug. If done correctly, the place where the last coil ends can hardly be detected. For pictures of one-stick baskets, see photographs number 4, 9, 12, 13 and 16.

The outer wall of the basket is made of sedge root, worked very close together in order to hide the willow, so that it will not show through. Each time a new sedge root is added, it is cut so it overlaps the previous sedge root and then tucked under the stitch. The willow  withes are overlapped too, as shown, but not tucked under. They are bound together by the sedge roots, the flat side of which is always turned against the willow withes.

As the walls of the basket rise, you can add different colored designs to the side by using black-stained bulrush roots for black patterns, and red-colored redbud twigs for red patterns. Illustrations of many different basket patterns are shown in this book.

Triple-Stick Coil Basket

This is also called the three-stick coil basket, and is started as already shown for the single-stick basket in illustrations a through g.

(h) Shown here is the beginning of the three willow coiled basket, with three willows being inserted into the knot of sedge roots instead of only one, as in the basket on the opposite page.

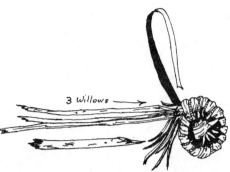

(i) As the three-willow coil is continued, the sedge root is woven into and around the coil with the aid of an awl with a sharp point making the holes for it (see photograph 24). Notice that the end of the sedge root is sharp-pointed to be able to fit through the awl-made holes. As the coil increases and the basket increases in size, new willows with sharpened ends and a new sedge root must be added to the beginning coil, the sharp points of each old willow being wedged together with the sharp point of a new

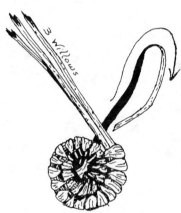

willow and then wrapped tightly. Two of the willows are placed on the root, one in and one outside, while the third and usually smaller willow is put on the top of the other two. Once the three willows are held this way, they are coiled together with the sedge root, which holds them tightly in its grip as it is threaded through each hole between the willows with the aid of the awl. The completion of the basket is continued as described for the one-stick coiled basket. You keep wetting the sedge root with your fingers dipped in water as you weave.

If the three-stick basket is done well and tight enough, it will hold water. In the old days, such baskets were used for boiling water in, using hot rocks dropped into the water in the basket to make it boil and cook mush or other food.

The finishing coil on a three-stick coil basket is done in a similar way to that done on the single-stick, except that the three willows are shaved off gradually into sharp points a little separated from each other so that the coil will come smoothly to an end, bound tightly by the sedge root until the point where the end is made is hardly seen. This is a careful molding operation, in which the transition to the end from the three willows in the coil is done evenly so that the top is smooth and even-looking.

Photograph No. 9 shows a number of coiled baskets. The two on the left and lower left are one-stick coiled baskets with arrow-head type designs. The two on the right are three-stick coiled gift baskets with old-time designs. Notice how tightly bound and even the coils appear. This is due to painstakingly careful work in putting these baskets together. Photo by Brooks Otis

(NOTE: All baskets on color plates, pages 34 and 35, are 3-stick coil types, except the beaded baskets.)

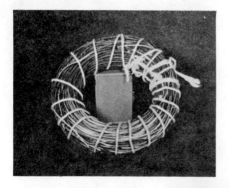

(10) A coil of redbud withes, scraped to an even size and tied for storage. Redbud is found in the interior Coast Ranges and in the Sierra foothills.

(11) A coil of sedge roots, untied and ready to be used. A bowl of water is usually kept handy for dipping the fingers in order to keep the sedge roots damp while they are being worked.

(12) One stick coil ceremonial basket with beads, made by a Medicine Woman. Notice unusual design motif made by using black-dyed bulrush roots.

(13) One stick coil canoe basket partially worked and showing large single willow withe used in the coil.

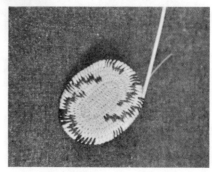

A. Bottom view of beaded 1-stick coiled basket with triangle design. Done by Lydia Fort, Lake County.

B. Flat feather basket with large star-flower form in center, decorated with cut and polished pieces of clam shell; mallard and meadowlark feathers. Made by Suzanne Holder, Upper Lake.

C. A round, medium-sized feather basket with zig-zag design, using mallard, oriole and meadowlark feathers. Made by Suzanne Holder, Upper Lake.

D. Side view of a medium-deep feather basket that has a step-like triangle design and sea-shell trim; mallard and meadowlark feathers. By Mrs. Annie Boon, Lake County

E. Shallow blue and yellow feather basket having a round bluish-green center; has handle. By Mrs. Susie Billie, Hopland.

F. Partially finished purple and reddish-brown basket of pheasant feathers made by Elsie Allen.

G. Blue and white beaded basket with a triangle-flower pattern. By Annie Lake, Redwood Valley.

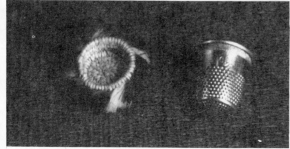

H. Midget feather basket of green mallard and yellow meadowlark feathers. By Elsie Allen

(14) Detail of bottom of wicker-weave twine basket, showing intricate nature of weave (above).

(15) Detail of finish of coil on the top of a three-stick coil basket, showing how three willows are gradually narrowed in size until they mold evenly into the top, while being woven to the coil below with the aid of an awl (pictured below).

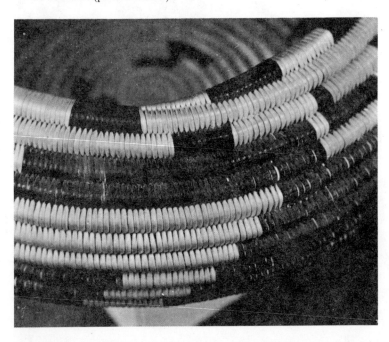

V

POMO FEATHER BASKETS

The beautiful Pomo Feather Baskets in the old days were made almost exclusively to be given as gifts to important or very much revered people. So much work went into these baskets that their value today is almost priceless, and any that are for sale usually start at around a thousand dollars.

Feathers of the meadowlark, mallard, pheasant, woodpecker and oriole were added, but any beautiful feathers may be used. Green mallard duck feathers were sometimes used in following a black design; yellow or white meadowlark feathers were used for a contrasting design in a basket; and red feathers of a small woodpecker were added here and there in a design for brilliant color that never fades.

The three-stick coil basket is the only one used to make a feather basket. When feathers are to be used in a design, they are first dried flat on paper with the skin attached. The lower end of each feather is then scraped clean with a knife to make sure all foreign material is removed from it. (If you need to store them for any length of time, keep feathers from moths by storing them in airtight cans with mothballs.)

To attach the feathers while weaving a basket, slide the pointed end onto the willows at a 45 degree angle, toward the left, between the sedge roots; then pull the sedge root tight so that the feather is gripped firmly in the stitch and on top of the two or three willows, with the beautiful color showing. The feathers are allowed to overlap each other and are carefully arranged to form designs, such as those shown in Color

Plates I and II, pages 34 and 35. This added ornamentation requires much more time to accomplish, and greatly enhances the beauty of the basket, adding to its value considerably.

In the old days, the Pomo shot birds with bows and arrows or trapped them in order to get feathers. The great red topknot of the Pileated Woodpecker was particularly in demand because of its brilliant unfading color. Today, however, most birds are protected by law, so feathers must be gathered from birds found dead of natural causes. Ask your friends to be on the lookout for such birds, especially all those that have colorful feathers which might be used in baskets.

Photograph 16 shows a number of thimble baskets, with two of them smaller than a dime, and requiring very delicate finger work. All are one-stick coiled baskets, and are usually given as gifts to indicate the skill of the maker. The one on the left is a round basket. Next is a tiny canoe basket. Third is a thimble-sized feather basket. Fourth is a beaded basket, and the last two are plain little finger baskets. Photo by Brooks Otis

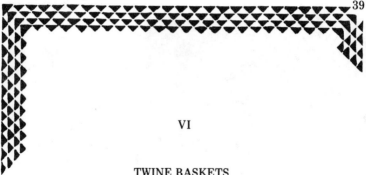

VI

TWINE BASKETS

Twine baskets are the most ancient of all baskets. There are some forms of twine baskets that no modern basket-maker knows how to make. The art of making them is lost. Twine baskets are generally more utility-type baskets, such as carrying baskets, storage baskets, winnowing baskets, and so forth. It is rarely possible to make them as beautiful as the coiled baskets. Some tribes have only twined baskets and never learned how to make coiled baskets.

Number 1 Twine Basket

This uses two roots, interwoven between each willow, and forms the common twine basket. The following photographs show the beginning and ending steps.

As sedge roots are inserted around willows, they are dampened by fingers dipped in water to make the roots supple.

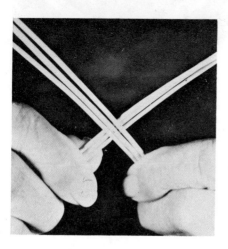

(17) This basket starts by holding three willows at right angles across three other willows, as shown.

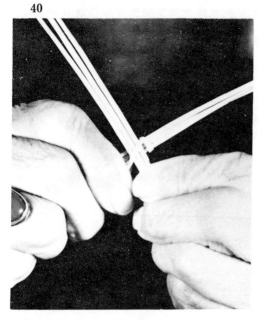

(18) Two sedge roots are tied around the two sets of willows to hold them together, keeping flat part of sedge roots against the willows.

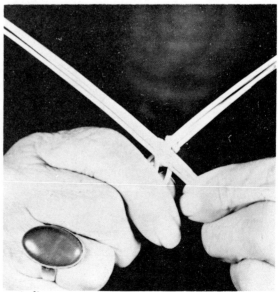

(19) Continue winding sedge roots around second set of three willows.

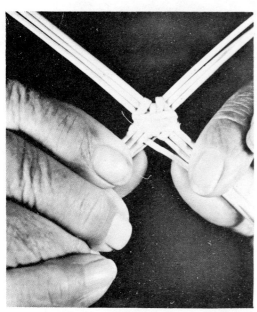

(20) Criss-cross sedge roots across the center of crossed willows, putting the sedge roots around the 4th set of three willows so that each of the four sides is bound.

(21) As pictured below, you now wind around and under all four sets of willows.

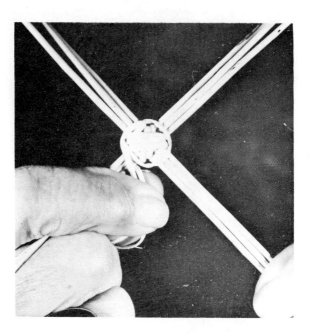

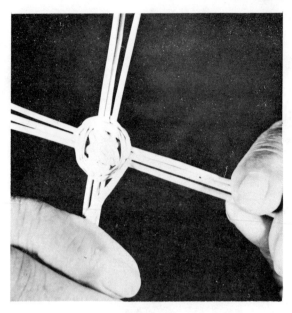

(22) In the photograph above, the sedge roots now go between two willows on the inside.

(23) In the photograph below, the sedge roots go between two willows on the outside.

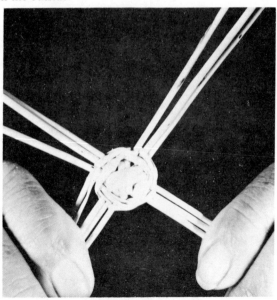

(24) Shows awl being used to punch hole between willow and sedge root for insertion of new willow into center of basket, as new willows are now to be added to circle of the coil.

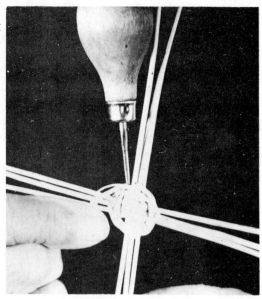

(25) New willows are shown here being added as spokes to circle of basket, each being put in by punching hole with awl in center. Each willow is trimmed on the end to make a sharp point to fit into hole. The two sedge roots are then wrapped around willows from opposite sides to lock them in place. This picture shows the appearance from the inner side of the basket.

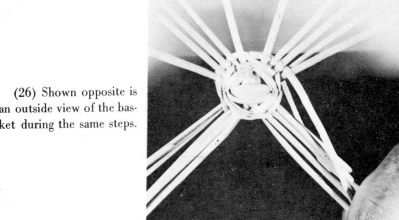

(26) Shown opposite is
an outside view of the basket during the same steps.

(27) Below is a twine winnowing basket partly finished to show the
weave and design being worked by changing sedge roots in one part of
the circle to redbud twigs to produce a red color design. The basket has
been continued by steadily weaving around the circle. Notice two willow
ridges where willow has taken place of sedge roots in weave. Some baskets are made entirely of willows. See Photographs 51 and 52.

(28) Same twine winnowing basket, showing the weave as seen from the inside. Notice that the redbud twigs are much thicker than the sedge roots. There are also willow ridges put around this basket to give it strength, the willow in such places being substituted for the sedge roots in part of the weave.

(29) Finished number 1 twine basket below.

(30)(Opposite page) Shows the finished appearance of two twined baskets, one on left, which is a No. 3-type twine basket, and one on upper right, which is a No. 1 twine basket. Both of these are contrasted with the 3-stick coiled basket with tufts of woodpecker feathers shown on the lower right. Notice that the twined baskets are finished rather roughly, by simply cutting off willow spokes within about a quarter inch of the top of the basket. The sedge root is ended by trimming the end to a point and tying the point to the basket at end. The basket shapes are regulated as you weave them by expanding circles of sedge roots if you wish basket to bow outward or tightening circles of sedge roots if you wish basket to constrict. Designs are put on by using black-dyed bulrush roots or reddish redbud roots for either black and/or red designs. Each has to be carefully worked into the overall plan of the basket. Many designs are shown in this book, but it is good to use your imagination to make your own designs.

Number 2 Twine Basket

This also uses two sedge roots, but with interweaving between the two willows—that is, one root goes up, while the other goes down. On the next round from the beginning, you work the opposite two willows by interweaving them. Continue to alternate with the opposite two willows on every round.

Number 3 Twine Basket

This is done the same as number 1, only an extra willow is held as you interweave the basket. This is put on by weaving the sedge root over and under this willow, then the same stick as number 1 continues; then over and under this extra willow again, and proceed with the same stick through the willows. Repeat. A basket of this type is shown in photograph number 30. This type of basket is not often made today, and is nearly a lost art.

Number 4 Twine Basket—Lattice Weave

This is also known as a sieve-basket, because that is what it is used for when leaching (pouring water over) pounded acorns to take the acid out of them.

This basket is made the same as number 3, only each part of the basket, as it is built up, is spread far enough apart to make it work like a sieve. The two photographs on the next page show how to make this basket, after the usual beginning already illustrated.

(31)(Top opposite page) This shows sifter twine basket with lattice weave. This basket is started with five willows crossing five other willows. After the sedge roots have started, a willow is used to form the main circle or coil while sedge roots tie it on to the spoke willows. First, one sedge root goes around willow on outside and then between each spoke to draw the circular willow tight to the spokes.

(32)(Bottom opposite page) Shows close-up of lattice weave.

Most lattice weave baskets need a stronger top than the usual type of twine basket because they get more strenuous handling. To make this strong top, you do the preliminary finishing of the basket in the usual way with the spoke willows being cut off about a quarter of an inch above the weave. You then take a willow that is long enough to go clear around the top of the basket and cut it so the two ends overlap about an inch. Trim these two ends to a point so they can fit together as

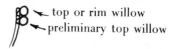

shown, and lash them tightly at this point with sedge roots at the same time beginning to lash the willow together as a rim for the top of the basket, putting this rim inside the ends of the spoke willows which have been trimmed off around the top of the basket, as shown. All should be tightly lashed to finish basket. (See photographs number 4 and 51.)

top or rim willow
preliminary top willow

Lattice weave baskets are very decorative as well as useful, and can be used to hold many objects big enough not to slip through the weave, or to simply hang on a wall as decorations.

(33) The Author with a Baby Basket

Photo by Robert Cooper

VII

BABY BASKETS AND BABY DOLL BASKETS ("SICKA")

Baby and baby doll baskets (the latter for small girls to play with), are made in essentially the same way, except the smaller basket has fewer willows. A completed baby basket is shown held by Elsie Allen (33) on opposite page.

Fresh willow is usually gathered for use in making the baby basket. Each willow twig is scraped and prepared (as already described on page 18) and tied in a half circle (as shown in photograph 34), usually in bundles of five (but three are often used for a baby doll basket). This starts part of the frame of a baby basket, and the willows are wrapped with cloth to protect them and left bent this way for about a week, depending on the weather, waiting a shorter time for dry weather and longer time for wet weather. If aged willows are to be used, first soak them in water to soften them and then shape and dry again.

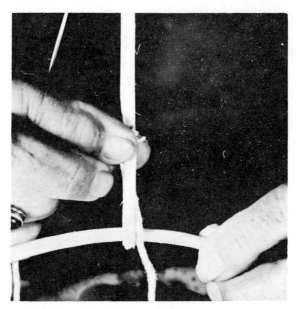

A medium-sized cotton string is used in baby baskets for weaving, instead of the usual sedge roots. To begin, your plan is to weave 29 to 32 curved willows together, all as the center of the bottom of the curve, or U-shape, using a straight willow as a frame for strength. The weave is begun by holding the straight and curved willows against each other, and placing the string in position for the first tie (see photograph 35 above).

The weave with string is done by holding the one willow in the left hand, and with your right hand taking the string with a knot at the end, holding it to the willow, and wrapping it around both sides of the straight willow to hold it tight to the frame (curved) willow, using a big sock needle to thread the string (see photograph 36 at right).

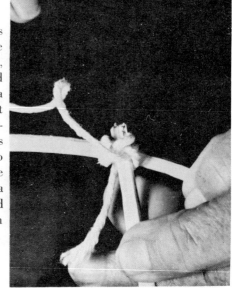

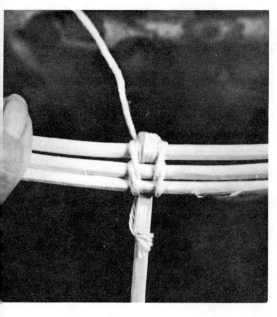

(37) Shows how you tie second and third willows onto the frame. The needle is run around between the two new willows of frame to tie them to the crosspiece willow, as shown. At each move in weaving, pull as tight as you can to fit string snugly to willows. This picture shows the basket frame from the inner side.

(38) Shows the same weaving as done from the outer side. Keep up this weaving until all the willows are tied together in this way across the bottom of the U.

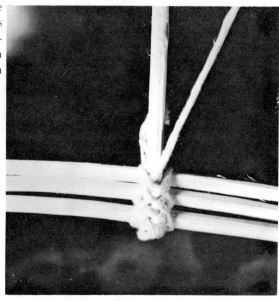

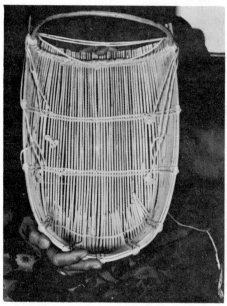

(39) This shows the finished basket, looking at it from the inside. Notice that each side of the basket has the willows of the frame tied together in five places to the cross-willows, making eleven such ties altogether. Notice also that four of the willows in this frame are longer than the other ones in the final frame, forming a knob on each side of the basket for use in hanging backstraps to if necessary. The cross-stitching of the willows on the side, which is to brace the basket, is done about 3 to 5 inches apart in a baby basket, but about 1½ to 2 inches apart in the baby doll basket.

The back of the basket is made by tying together in the same way as described before about 42 to 45 straight willows in a baby basket, or about 29 to 32 straight willows in a baby doll basket. As this is fitted to the U-shaped frame of the basket, it is necessary to turn the bottom ends of the willows up after soaking them in water for two days to make them bendable (as shown in picture 39) so they fit the U-shaped bottom of the frame. This back is then lashed to the frame with the string woven tightly around the connections.

An oak sapling is made into a circle to be lashed to the top. This rim or hoop is a shoot 43 inches long, uniform in size and thickness. The ends of this shoot are cut to slant and tied together to form a perfect smooth circle, whittled and overlapped to be 38 inches round. Place this circled shoot 1½ inches from the top of the four high willows and ½ inch from all the forty or so willows that form the basket. This hoop is wrapped with twine between every two willows and is held firm and secure. This is a protection for the baby's head in case the basket falls, and the hoop can also be covered with a skin or cloth to protect the baby from rain or sun. Corded strings on either side of the basket are tied to the walls to give fastening places for the cords or straps which lash the baby in place while he sits in the curved part of the basket and his feet dangle.

Comparison of Baby and Baby Doll Baskets

	No. of willows on sides	No. of willows on back	Length of side & bottom willows	Length of back willows
Baby basket	29-32	42-45	50 inches	about 21"
Baby doll basket	18-21	29-32	25 inches	11 inches

The braided leather or woven twine strap with which to hold the baby is generally 45" long. A braided twine eleven feet long is used to strap the baby into the basket, and a 6" braided twine is used to hold this strap firmly to the side. There are three pieces of twine, two pieces attached to the left side, one twine on the right side.

The Pomo name for the baby basket is "sicka."

(40) Below shows the back of the baby basket. Notice the strap used for carrying or for hanging from a tree. However, regular straps can be fastened to the basket to go around the shoulders and head of the mother so she can carry it easily.

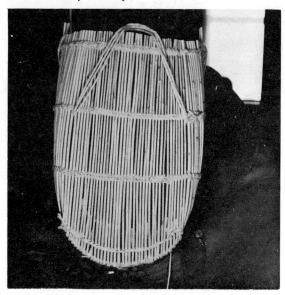

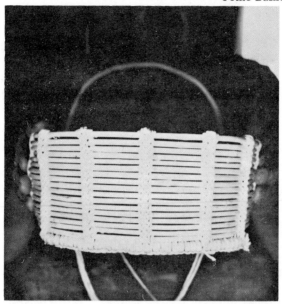

(41) A photograph of the bottom of a baby basket, showing the weave, which strengthens the willows in five places. It also shows how the willow withes are bent at the bottom of the back to add strength to this part of the back.

(42) This is a close-up of the binding together of the willow withes on the inside of the baby basket.

(43) Above is a close-up of the same binding on the outside of the
baby basket.

When a baby is put into one of these baskets, it is, of course,
swaddled in a warm blanket or other soft warm material in order to
keep it comfortable. Such baskets made wonderful carriers for the mother to use in both travel and work. The mother could work with the baby
on her back, or could use the back strap to hang the baby from the
branch of a tree near where she was working. Feathers or shells or other
objects were often dangled from the top ring of the baby basket to give
the baby something to play with and amuse itself while the mother was
working.

A well-done baby basket was a tribute to and a sign of mother's
love and her desire to keep her baby happy and comfortable in all conditions. It was also admirable training for the baby, as its back was kept
straight and firm, and it was raised up to a high position where it could
observe and begin to understand all the interesting things happening in
the world about it.

▲▲▲▲▲▲▲▲

VIII

CANOE BASKETS

These baskets are actually coiled baskets, done in the same general way as already described for coiled baskets, except at the beginning it is necessary to make them long and canoe-shaped instead of round. They are very useful in holding objects whenever the place on which they sit is long and narrow. There are two kinds of canoe baskets, the one-stick canoe basket and the three-stick canoe basket, just as in regular coiled baskets.

One-Stick Canoe Basket

The willows need to be soaked beforehand so they can be easily bent to start this basket. Photograph 44 below shows you how to weave together two short willows and a long willow (on top), holding them together with your left hand while you begin weaving them together at the bottom, or beginning with the sedge root in your right hand. Keep wetting your fingers as you wrap and weave with the sedge root. With your right hand, wrap the end of the sedge root around the long willow and bend it around towards you, catching the two short willows to the long willow (as shown).

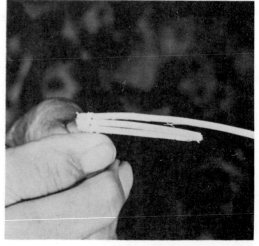

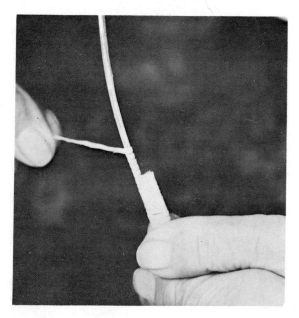

(45) Above, the sedge root is wrapped around the three willows until you come to the end of the two short willows and still have the long willow sticking out. This long willow is then wrapped around with sedge root alone for a little ways.

(46) (opposite) This shows how the long willow is now bent back along the side of the short willows and the awl is used (as shown) to weave the three willows together with the root. Be sure to make the point of the root sharp so that it can be easily pushed into the tiny holes made by the awl. To attach a new root to the old root, put the new root in the hole next to the old root. Pull the old root through under the willow; then cut it. The new root is then held snugly in place.

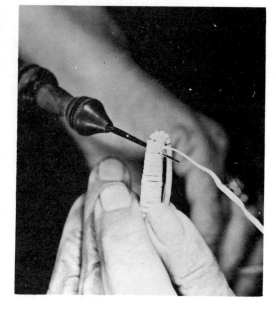

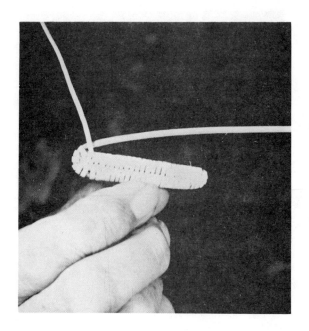

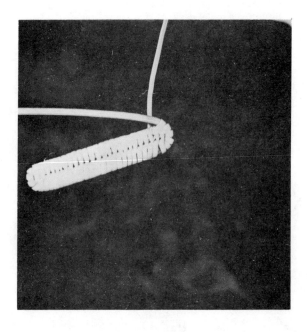

(47) (Top opposite page) This shows the inside face of the start of a canoe basket, with the long willow bent back for the second time and continuing to be wrapped with sedge root as the canoe-shaped coil continues.

(48) (Bottom opposite page) This shows the outer face of the same weave as above. Notice that when the willow's end is reached, it is trimmed to a fine point and the next willow is also made into a point so that the points overlap and are tied tightly together by the weaving of the sedge root around them and to the next part of the willow below. This is continued until the basket is finished.

(49) (Below) Here we see the inside of the completed canoe basket to show continuation of weave. The shaping of this basket is done as in the coil baskets described previously; by widening circles of willow just slightly as you weave the lower sides of the basket, and tightening them just slightly as you weave the top sides where the top begins to curve in. The top and final rim of the basket is made as already described under coil baskets, by trimming willow to a slant, and weaving to the end over this slant and cutting off the end of the sedge root after the final knot is tied tightly.

(50) Shows the weave
on the bottom and outer
side of the completed basket to show how it looks
from that side.

Seed beads are often used in the one-stick basket all around by
stringing a bead through the root on the outside of the basket with each
stitch of the weave. Designs are put on the basket's sides as already described. The three-stick canoe basket (see below) may have seed beads
worked into the basket in a more scattered pattern if desired.

Three-Stick Canoe Basket

This is started in the same way as the above basket, except that
three long willows are used with one short willow to start. The length
of the basket is determined by the length of the one short willow.

To start, you hold the three long willows in your left hand—not
side by side, but with one willow on top of the other two willows. The
fourth willow is short and is held in place below the three long willows.
The top part of the fourth willow is slit in the center and the root is put
in this hole to start weaving. Be sure the round part of the root is on
top, the flat side against the willow. This root is wrapped towards you,
around the four willows one by one until you come to the end of the
short willow. Then you continue to wrap the three long willows and
bend the three willows (previously soaked in water to make them supple) to make your turn. This is all done at the same time, the weaving
and bending. Now continue to weave the other side with the three willows and the top willow only. Continue and finish the top part of the
basket plain or with a design.

(51) Shown here is Elsie's mother, Mrs. Annie Burke, with two great grandchildren, Rozanne and Jacqueline Mitchell. The baskets hanging on the wall above Mrs. Burke are all lattice weave twine baskets. They are, from left to right: winnowing basket, all-willow work basket of number 1 twine type, small winnowing basket, fish trap, baby doll basket, and large all-willow storage or work basket. (All-willow baskets are made by substituting thin willow withes for sedge roots.)

(52) Shown here is Elsie Allen and her mother, Annie Burke, in 1949, with many examples of fine Pomo basketry. Top row from left to right shows large, lattice weave twine storage basket, a very large twine winnowing basket of regular weave, and another large, lattice weave twine storage basket.

Second row, from left to right, shows a one-stick coiled basket for storing food, an all-willow wicker work basket for holding thread, socks, mending, etc.; a small number 1 type twine basket for cooking acorn meal; a small lattice weave twine basket for leaching acorns or holding seaweed, etc.; a large number 1 twine basket for cooking acorns, etc.; a lattice weave, twine basket for storage; a small number 1 twine storage basket; an all-willow miniature storage basket of number 1 twine type; a one-stick coiled basket for use as a platter; a Yurok baby doll basket.

Third or bottom row: a large all-willow wicker work storage basket; a one-stick coiled canoe basket with arrowhead design; a Papago basket with turtle design on it; a one-stick large coiled basket for gift-holding; a Papago basket with bird design on it; a non-Pomo basket with whirling design; an all-willow miniature storage basket of number 1 twine type.

Below, in front, is an unfinished basket of number 1 twine type, showing whirling design and numerous spokes of willows.

(53) This is another picture of Mrs. Burke, holding a large wicker twine basket and an acorn pounder of ancient times made out of black chert.

ACKNOWLEDGMENTS

All of us here at Naturegraph enjoyed doing our part in assisting in the preparation of this fine book.

The cover was designed by Greg Twain using the two beautiful Pomo Indian baskets painted by Douglas Andrews. Tony Shearer drew the illustrations of the steps in weaving of coil baskets on pages 26 through 29. The typesetting; and all other illustrations including the awl, the four main plants used in basketweaving and the designs on the Section headings and endings were done by Teddi Heater. The valuable old photographs were contributed by the author and the photographers indicated when known. The black and white photographs showing the steps for basketweaving of twine, baby, and canoe baskets and the color pictures on pages 34 and 35 were taken by Vinson Brown.

Beaded basket made by Author's Grandmother in 1916; lower beaded basket made by the Author.

SOME OTHER BOOKS BY NATUREGRAPH

A BAG OF BONES, *by Marcelle Masson.* Fascinating legends of the Wintu Indians of northern California, as told absorbingly by an "old one," Grant Towendolly, who was one of the last of the Wintu shamans. 130 pages.

THE POMO INDIANS OF CALIFORNIA AND THEIR NEIGHBORS, *by Vinson Brown, illustrated by Douglas Andrews.* A full-color map designed with paintings of Indian life shows the old trails and villages. There are 70 illustrations in this 64 page book, including 12 photographs. The text is interestingly told.

LORD OF THE DAWN—Quetzalcoatl, *by Tony Shearer.* The story of ancient Mexico and her great prophet, the Plumed Serpent, written in poetic prose. A look at the Indian past, telling of great lost cities, temples and pyramids. Includes 7 color plates, and 200 pages illustrated by the author.

THE WINTUN INDIANS OF CALIFORNIA AND THEIR NEIGHBORS, *by Peter M. Knudtson.* This ethnographic account gives the reader an accurate mental picture of Wintun cultural life as it existed in prewhite times. Full-color map included.

VOICES OF EARTH AND SKY, *by Vinson Brown, illustrated by Tony Shearer.* A remarkable, personal study of the vision life of the native Americans and their culture heroes. Interwoven with Hiawatha, Sweet Medicine, White Buffalo Calf Maiden, Quetzacoatl, and many more. 180 pages.

INDIAN TALK—Hand Signals of the North American Indians, *by Iron Eyes Cody.* For all ages. Contains 80 pages and over 150 illustrations of Plains Tribes sign language.

TAPESTRIES IN SAND—The Spirit of Indian Sandpainting, *by David Villaseñor.* 16 pages of beautiful color plates, 112 pages in all. The author, a part Otomi Indian, was adopted as a boy into the Navajo tribe and learned sandpainting from the medicine men. The ancient art and its inner meanings are warmly described.

See these and other Naturegraph books at your local book store or send to Naturegraph Publishers, Inc., Happy Camp, CA 96039 for catalog.